COMPREHENSION SKILLS

CONTEXT

LEVEL F

Linda Ward Beech

Tara McCarthy

Donna Townsend

STECK-VAUGHN
ELEMENTARY · SECONDARY · ADULT · LIBRARY

A Harcourt Company

www.steck-vaughn.com

Editorial Director:	Diane Schnell
Project Editor:	Anne Souby
Associate Director of Design:	Cynthia Ellis
Design Manager:	Cynthia Hannon
Media Researcher:	Christina Berry
Production:	Rusty Kay
Cover Illustration:	Stephanie Carter
Cover Production:	Alan Klemp
Photographs:	©PhotoDisc (sheep); ©Stockbyte (yarn)

ISBN 0-7398-2658-1

Using context means learning a new word by looking at the words surrounding it. In this book you will learn new words by looking at the context.

What is context? Suppose you were in a house in the city. If someone told you to get some wool, you might go to the store and buy wool yarn. But if you were on a farm, you might get the wool from sheep. In the context of a city, people think of a store when they think of wool. In the context of a farm, people think of sheep when they think of wool.

What Is Context?

Context means all the words in a sentence or all the sentences in a paragraph. In a sentence all the words together make up the context. In a paragraph all the sentences together make up the context. You can use the context to figure out the meaning of unknown words.

Try It!

The following paragraph has a word that you may not know. See whether you can use the context (the sentences and other words in the paragraph) to decide what the word means.

> Scientists are very concerned about **famine** in many parts of the world today. Thousands of people are starving because they cannot grow enough crops. Lack of rain and poor farming methods sometimes cause the problem. Often the problem is that there are too many people for the land to support.

If you don't know what **famine** means, you can decide by using the context. The paragraph contains these words:

Clue: thousands of people are starving

Clue: cannot grow enough crops

Clue: lack of rain

Clue: too many people

Find these clues in the paragraph and circle them. What words do you think of when you read the clues? Write the words below:

_____

Did you write *hunger* or a similar word? The context clue words tell you that **famine** is a lack of food.

Using What You Know

Below are some paragraphs with words left out. Read the paragraphs. Look at the context. Then fill in the blanks with words about you.

I once took a walk in the _____ . There I saw _____ and _____ . A beautiful _____ went by me like a _____ .

My best friend and I like to go to _____ . We go there in the _____ . When we are there, I _____ , but my friend likes to _____ .

My favorite movie is _____ . I like this movie because it is _____ and _____ . I would like to take _____ to see this movie.

The worst thing in the world is _____ . If I could, I would _____ this thing. I would find a way to _____ it.

I was playing _____ . The other player _____ , but I was able to _____ . I _____ the game.

Working with Context

This book asks questions that you can answer by using context clues in paragraphs. There are two kinds of paragraphs. The paragraphs in the first part of this book have blank spaces in them. You can use the context clues in the paragraphs to decide which words should go in each space. Here is an example:

> Baboons live in groups. Usually there are about sixty ___1___ in the group, but there may be as many as two hundred or as few as ten. Living in a tribe ___2___ the baboons from their enemies.

_C_ 1. **A.** jars   **B.** museums   **C.** individuals   **D.** patients

_____ 2. **A.** hides   **B.** safeguards   **C.** leads   **D.** grazes

Look at the answer choices for blank 1. Try putting each choice in the paragraph to see which one makes the most sense. Treat the paragraph as a puzzle. Determine which pieces don't fit and which piece fits best. The paragraph tells about baboons living in groups. It doesn't make sense to say that there are sixty *jars, museums,* or *patients. Individuals* (answer **C**) is the only choice that makes sense in this paragraph. Now try to answer question 2 on your own.

The paragraphs in the second part of this book are different. For these you figure out the meaning of a word that is printed in **dark letters** in the paragraph. Here is an example:

> Many vines have long **clusters** of sweet-smelling flowers. Vines will climb posts and other objects. They are often planted for their beauty and shade.

In this paragraph, the word in dark type is **clusters**. Find the context clues, and treat the paragraph as a puzzle. Then choose a word that means the same as **clusters**.

_____ 3. In this paragraph, the word **clusters** means
     A. animals   **C.** drinks
     B. stems   **D.** bunches

To check your answers, turn to page 60.

How to Use This Book

This book has 25 units. In units 1 through 12, you will read stories with blank spaces where words have been left out. Use the context of each story to help you choose words to fill the blanks. In units 13 through 25, the stories have words printed in dark letters. Use the context of each story to help you choose the correct meaning for the word in dark letters.

When you finish reading each story and answering the questions about it, check your answers by looking at pages 61 and 62. Write the number of correct answers in the score box at the top of the page.

Hints

- ◆ Look for context clues while you are reading the stories. Ask yourself, Where is this story happening? Who is in the story? What is the story about?
- ◆ When you finish reading, look at each answer choice carefully. Try to put each answer choice into the paragraph. The paragraph is like a puzzle. Which words don't fit? Which one fits best?
- ◆ If you cannot find the answer the first time, look back at the story. Then try the answer choices again.

Challenge

Read each story and choose the correct answer choice. Then try to write sentences of your own using the correct answer choices.

Writing

On pages 30–31 and 58–59, there are paragraphs for you to complete. Write a word or sentence that makes sense in each paragraph. You will find suggested answers on page 60, but your answers may be very different.

The head of the baleen whale is about one third its ___**1**___ length. The whale's diet ___**2**___ only of the tiniest sea creatures. The whale strains these creatures through plates in its mouth.

_____ **1. A.** shark   **B.** total   **C.** motor   **D.** ocean

_____ **2. A.** consists   **B.** reduces   **C.** improves   **D.** knows

---

Most people think of wood as a building material. However, it is also used to make paper. Machines grind the wood into ___**3**___, which is then mixed with a type of glue and rolled flat into big sheets. Now some ___**4**___ paper can also be made into new paper so not as much wood is needed.

_____ **3. A.** toothpicks   **B.** pulp   **C.** hardness   **D.** gravel

_____ **4. A.** recycled   **B.** labeled   **C.** crumpled   **D.** burned

---

The ___**5**___ purpose of the song "Yankee Doodle" was to show American soldiers in the Revolution as silly and weak. But after a time, the Yankees made the song their own. They even sang it together in ___**6**___ as they marched into battle.

_____ **5. A.** original   **B.** casual   **C.** slight   **D.** dry

_____ **6. A.** concern   **B.** cradles   **C.** bloom   **D.** chorus

---

The Wright Brothers would not stop trying to fly. They ___**7**___ built a successful plane. They made a little money. They never ___**8**___ much.

_____ **7. A.** suddenly   **B.** eventually   **C.** dimly   **D.** falsely

_____ **8. A.** fished   **B.** ran   **C.** profited   **D.** sang

When you write, you may need to correct an ___**9**___. Then you can thank Hyman Lipman. In 1858 he had the ___**10**___ to put erasers on pencils.

_____ **9.** **A.** inch   **B.** origin   **C.** aim   **D.** error

_____**10.** **A.** inspiration   **B.** failure   **C.** point   **D.** speech

---

An ___**11**___ in the theater doesn't have wings. This term refers to a person, usually ___**12**___, who gives money to help put on a play or show.

_____**11.** **A.** actor   **B.** enemy   **C.** angel   **D.** island

_____**12.** **A.** wealthy   **B.** homeless   **C.** fierce   **D.** small

---

One company tested moon rock by roasting it. The company then decided to make ___**13**___ from the crumbled rock. This material turned out to be stronger than that made of Earth rocks. Moon rock is more ___**14**___ than Earth rock.

_____**13.** **A.** trees   **B.** concrete   **C.** fruit   **D.** miracles

_____**14.** **A.** sweet   **B.** empty   **C.** risky   **D.** durable

---

James Michener was a famous author who loved taking walks all his life. One of his favorite places to walk was through ___**15**___ pine tree forests. He liked to walk alone in the evenings. Occasionally he ___**16**___ the sun setting through the trees.

_____**15.** **A.** dirty   **B.** crowded   **C.** fragrant   **D.** smelly

_____**16.** **A.** arrested   **B.** searched   **C.** glimpsed   **D.** wrestled

The world's rain forests are being destroyed. The greatest ___**1**___ to rain forests come from humans. They strip away the trees. This leaves the land ___**2**___.

_____ **1. A.** trips   **B.** threats   **C.** praises   **D.** rides

_____ **2. A.** green   **B.** full   **C.** cool   **D.** barren

---

There were many African American cowboys in the Old West. Will Pickett was one. He was the ___**3**___ of a rodeo event. In this event a cowboy ___**4**___ a bull to the ground by its horns.

_____ **3. A.** garden   **B.** money   **C.** creator   **D.** fort

_____ **4. A.** wrestles   **B.** owns   **C.** pats   **D.** scares

---

Tito Puente is a composer and ___**5**___. He is a fine drummer. He gave many listeners their ___**6**___ to Latin American music in the 1950s.

_____ **5. A.** audience   **B.** entertainer   **C.** flyer   **D.** swimmer

_____ **6. A.** good-bye   **B.** introduction   **C.** index   **D.** address

---

Maya Angelou was a top ___**7**___ in school. She graduated with honors. She writes poems and novels. She uses her ___**8**___ as an author to tell about women.

_____ **7. A.** winner   **B.** teacher   **C.** student   **D.** astronaut

_____ **8. A.** dream   **B.** vacation   **C.** editor   **D.** talent

Saudi Arabia is a desert country where ___9___ is always a problem. Some years ago the king planned to tow a huge ___10___ from the South Pole to supply his country with water.

_____ 9. **A.** chocolate   **B.** drought   **C.** camel   **D.** fashion

_____ 10. **A.** fish   **B.** fountain   **C.** leaf   **D.** iceberg

More than one hundred years ago, Charles Babbage drew a ___11___ for a machine that could calculate. If built, the ___12___ would have been the first computer.

_____ 11. **A.** diagram   **B.** bet   **C.** cake   **D.** problem

_____ 12. **A.** water   **B.** device   **C.** book   **D.** game

Watching TV can be ___13___. But after a while, you might feel bored. That's the time to come up with your own ___14___. Make a new friend, start a hobby, or learn a skill.

_____ 13. **A.** general   **B.** housework   **C.** usual   **D.** relaxing

_____ 14. **A.** elevator   **B.** sunshine   **C.** recreation   **D.** recipes

Some lawmakers think there should be laws about false teeth. They want these ___15___ teeth to have a special ___16___ to identify the owner in case of accident.

_____ 15. **A.** clean   **B.** sharp   **C.** open   **D.** artificial

_____ 16. **A.** numeral   **B.** river   **C.** tooth   **D.** brush

It has been said that *Idaho* means "gem of the mountains" in the Shoshoni language. This is ___1___ not true. People believed this story about the ___2___ , but the word does not mean anything in any language.

_____ **1.** **A.** absolutely   **B.** softly   **C.** proudly   **D.** loudly

_____ **2.** **A.** danger   **B.** definition   **C.** series   **D.** mining

A bellmaker was hired in 1828 to replace the cracked Liberty Bell. A ___3___ of his fee was the old bell. But he left the bell behind. He ___4___ taking it as too much trouble.

_____ **3.** **A.** small   **B.** copper   **C.** portion   **D.** bandit

_____ **4.** **A.** regarded   **B.** bought   **C.** rang   **D.** scared

The skin is the largest organ of a human being. It is the first line of ___5___ against bumps, dirt, and germs. The skin is waterproof and keeps valuable ___6___ inside the body.

_____ **5.** **A.** retreat   **B.** defense   **C.** unhappiness   **D.** hunger

_____ **6.** **A.** poisons   **B.** dust   **C.** sunshine   **D.** fluids

George Washington did not win the first ___7___ he ran in. Before he became President, he ran for office in Virginia. He was ___8___ twice.

_____ **7.** **A.** game   **B.** election   **C.** horse   **D.** showing

_____ **8.** **A.** king   **B.** smiling   **C.** defeated   **D.** soon

In ancient times ____**9**____ in different parts of the world named the stars. In almost every ___**10**___, stars were named for animals.

_____ **9. A.** seas   **B.** astronomers   **C.** stars   **D.** meters

_____**10. A.** student   **B.** civilization   **C.** third   **D.** time

---

The first movie with a ___**11**___ about traveling to the moon was made in 1902 in France. In the film, moon walkers put up umbrellas to keep off the ___**12**___ of the sun.

_____**11. A.** check   **B.** camera   **C.** producer   **D.** plot

_____**12. A.** hobbies   **B.** rain   **C.** movie   **D.** rays

---

Deer know each other from the scent on the ___**13**___ of their hind legs. Each deer has a different scent. A ___**14**___ knows its mother by sniffing her hind legs.

_____**13. A.** shoes   **B.** trim   **C.** ankles   **D.** head

_____**14. A.** monkey   **B.** fawn   **C.** father   **D.** turn

---

The continents are slowly drifting apart. Since they are not ___**15**___, North and South America will one day ___**16**___ entirely. Then the ocean will flow between them.

_____**15. A.** clean   **B.** stationary   **C.** moving   **D.** land

_____**16. A.** name   **B.** reverse   **C.** separate   **D.** lock

UNIT 4

The kangaroo and the wombat keep their newborns very close after birth. Many of them raise their young in their ___1___ until the babies have ___2___ strength to leave.

_____ 1. **A.** farm **B.** tree **C.** steady **D.** pouch

_____ 2. **A.** no **B.** sufficient **C.** many **D.** national

A man named Richebourg was a spy in France nearly three hundred years ago. He was only 23 inches tall. He was most ___3___ when he was disguised as an ___4___ being carried by his nurse.

_____ 3. **A.** modern **B.** friendly **C.** successful **D.** French

_____ 4. **A.** infant **B.** extra **C.** armor **D.** owl

Cheese factories ___5___ many health inspections. Some people feel that the taste of cheese has gotten worse. It has been ___6___ by processes designed to make it safe.

_____ 5. **A.** remind **B.** require **C.** read **D.** milk

_____ 6. **A.** altered **B.** helped **C.** freed **D.** risen

Many people have an ___7___ of bats as bloodthirsty animals. This is not a true picture. Most bats live on a ___8___ of insects, flowers, or fruit.

_____ 7. **A.** answer **B.** action **C.** elevator **D.** image

_____ 8. **A.** diet **B.** plate **C.** tree **D.** bush

Steck-Vaughn • Comprehension Skills Series

Most animals have a bone __9__ in their feet like the toes of human feet. In the horse the number of toes has been __10__ to one. Its hoof is really its middle toenail.

_____ **9. A.** break   **B.** disease   **C.** structure   **D.** force

_____ **10. A.** reduced   **B.** polished   **C.** breaded   **D.** added

---

The right whale got its name because it floated after it died. This made it easier to peel off the blubber. It was the "right" whale to kill, so it became the __11__ target of hunters. This situation almost caused the whale's __12__.

_____ **11. A.** birth   **B.** few   **C.** winter   **D.** primary

_____ **12. A.** fat   **B.** trick   **C.** doom   **D.** question

---

A man named Bottineau lived in the eighteenth century. He had __13__ eyesight. He __14__ this on more than one hundred occasions. He could see ships coming into port up to four days before they arrived.

_____ **13. A.** serious   **B.** remarkable   **C.** weak   **D.** quiet

_____ **14. A.** regarded   **B.** turned   **C.** demonstrated   **D.** armed

---

Patricia McKissack puts in __15__ details about where her books take place. Sights, sounds, and smells __16__ in her descriptions.

_____ **15. A.** various   **B.** loud   **C.** hidden   **D.** dark

_____ **16. A.** spill   **B.** shout   **C.** march   **D.** mingle

Many movies show deserts as hot areas covered with sand ___1___. In real life the typical desert does look ___2___. But it is covered with rocks, not sand.

_____ 1. **A.** lakes   **B.** castles   **C.** sneezes   **D.** dunes

_____ 2. **A.** watery   **B.** cool   **C.** harsh   **D.** carpeted

---

Laws about using water to ___3___ crops go back to ancient times. Thousands of years ago, the Babylonians had many laws and ___4___ for the use of water.

_____ 3. **A.** irrigate   **B.** burn   **C.** park   **D.** destroy

_____ 4. **A.** rulers   **B.** regulations   **C.** families   **D.** phones

---

The coconut got its name from the Portuguese word *coco*. This word describes the ___5___ on the face of someone who is in pain. The "face" of the coconut seems to have this same ___6___ look.

_____ 5. **A.** scars   **B.** expression   **C.** love   **D.** teeth

_____ 6. **A.** smiling   **B.** partly   **C.** miserable   **D.** watch

---

The fruit of the banana plant takes three to five months to ___7___ completely. Bananas don't ripen ___8___ unless picked. This is why they are picked when they are still green.

_____ 7. **A.** talk   **B.** care   **C.** mature   **D.** cease

_____ 8. **A.** properly   **B.** tomorrow   **C.** bubbly   **D.** madly

The akee is a fruit that grows in the hot climate of the ___**9**___. It is not eaten ___**10**___. It is cooked the way a vegetable is. It tastes just like scrambled eggs.

_____ **9. A.** Arctic   **B.** ocean   **C.** tropics   **D.** fell

_____**10. A.** entirely   **B.** politely   **C.** bravely   **D.** raw

---

To make olive oil, the olives are first cut into large, ___**11**___ chunks and then pressed. The sweetest and most ___**12**___ oil comes from the first pressing.

_____**11. A.** sour   **B.** dirty   **C.** sugary   **D.** coarse

_____**12. A.** delicate   **B.** tiny   **C.** sifted   **D.** burned

---

Charles Kittering invented the electric self-starter in 1911. Before that, car engines had to be ___**13**___ by hand to get started. The electric self-starter ___**14**___ a person to sit in the car and simply push a button to start the car.

_____**13. A.** watered   **B.** lit   **C.** filled   **D.** cranked

_____**14. A.** removed   **B.** hit   **C.** enabled   **D.** pushed

---

Cheese is actually a form of milk that has begun to ___**15**___ and go sour. The "blue" in blue cheese is a result of ___**16**___ that begins to take over the food.

_____**15. A.** shine   **B.** fresh   **C.** drink   **D.** decay

_____**16. A.** mold   **B.** dye   **C.** people   **D.** dust

Mario Molina studied science. He did ____**1**___ about Earth's ozone layer. The ___**2**___ of his work led to a Nobel Prize.

_____ **1.** **A.** research   **B.** jobs   **C.** problems   **D.** professors

_____ **2.** **A.** ease   **B.** outcome   **C.** students   **D.** newspaper

---

There is a strong ___**3**___ between John Muir and forests. He had no ___**4**___ about speaking out. He got Congress to set aside land for national parks.

_____ **3.** **A.** need   **B.** association   **C.** trail   **D.** threat

_____ **4.** **A.** happiness   **B.** hesitation   **C.** rest   **D.** friends

---

Many people ___**5**___ that Columbus was the only person of his time who thought the world was round. But many others were also ___**6**___ of that fact, including the Spanish royal family.

_____ **5.** **A.** laugh   **B.** amount   **C.** assume   **D.** prevent

_____ **6.** **A.** stupid   **B.** confused   **C.** patient   **D.** aware

---

Harriet Beecher Stowe was a strong ___**7**___ of slavery. Her book *Uncle Tom's Cabin* had a great ___**8**___. It showed readers how bad slavery was.

_____ **7.** **A.** friend   **B.** writer   **C.** aunt   **D.** foe

_____ **8.** **A.** payments   **B.** agreement   **C.** influence   **D.** reader

William Enos did not have a driver's __**9**__. He could not operate a car. But he invented stop signs and one-way streets. He also wrote the first __**10**__ of traffic regulations.

_____ **9. A.** job   **B.** speed   **C.** license   **D.** ticket

_____ **10. A.** play   **B.** song   **C.** manual   **D.** street

One kind of caterpillar can __**11**__ itself. It puffs up its head and part of its body into a triangle that looks like a snake's head. When it __**12**__ a snake, it may scare away enemies.

_____ **11. A.** wrap   **B.** feed   **C.** disguise   **D.** climb

_____ **12. A.** mimics   **B.** sees   **C.** follows   **D.** chases

Ida Lewis, a light keeper's daughter, kept the light burning in the lighthouse at Lime Rock Light in Rhode Island. She was only 15 when she rescued four men from the sea. Their boat had __**13**__. This __**14**__ and others like it made her famous.

_____ **13. A.** sailed   **B.** won   **C.** capsized   **D.** floated

_____ **14. A.** woman   **B.** light   **C.** fiction   **D.** incident

Rachel Jackson did not want her husband Andrew to be a __**15**__ for President. She __**16**__ his decision to run for office, but she did not try to stop him.

_____ **15. A.** candidate   **B.** senator   **C.** voter   **D.** failure

_____ **16. A.** liked   **B.** regretted   **C.** halted   **D.** wished

In 1908 the president of an automobile company put on an exciting demonstration. He ____**1**___ the parts of three different cars. Then the cars were put back together. This showed that cars could be built with parts that were interchangeable. ____**2**___ each part could fit only the car it was made for.

_____ 1. **A.** melted   **B.** jumbled   **C.** waited   **D.** froze

_____ 2. **A.** Previously   **B.** Above   **C.** Beneath   **D.** Beside

The bagpipe is a musical instrument played in Scotland. It makes a lonely, ____**3**___ sound. One pipe plays the melody while the other three play low ____**4**___ notes.

_____ 3. **A.** moist   **B.** angry   **C.** forlorn   **D.** misty

_____ 4. **A.** sick   **B.** narrow   **C.** argue   **D.** bass

In the Middle Ages, a ____**5**___ did more than just cut hair. This person would often act as a doctor and perform ____**6**___ on sick people.

_____ 5. **A.** man   **B.** writer   **C.** barber   **D.** wife

_____ 6. **A.** operations   **B.** jokes   **C.** weddings   **D.** lights

People who can't use their arms or legs the way most others do are called ____**7**___. They learn to do things new ways. Adults who can't use their leg muscles might learn to drive a car using hand switches. Some people may learn how to cook while standing with ____**8**___.

_____ 7. **A.** tired   **B.** disabled   **C.** young   **D.** sir

_____ 8. **A.** tables   **B.** elevators   **C.** curbs   **D.** crutches

A sightseeing ___9___ of London always includes a look at Big Ben. Big Ben is neither a clock nor the tower that holds it. It is the bell that ___10___ every hour.

_____ **9. A.** shape **B.** dog **C.** tour **D.** lake

_____ **10. A.** breaks **B.** chimes **C.** cracks **D.** asks

Some Americans are ___11___ of the difference between England and Great Britain. It's a mistake to think that they are the same. England is only one part of the island of Great Britain. Great Britain is the large island that ___12___ England, Wales, and Scotland.

_____ **11. A.** upset **B.** wild **C.** ignorant **D.** sad

_____ **12. A.** leaves **B.** includes **C.** draws **D.** centers

Camels are known for their ___13___ to go for days and even weeks without water. But this is not because camels use their humps for water ___14___. The humps are all fat.

_____ **13. A.** capacity **B.** friends **C.** failing **D.** humor

_____ **14. A.** sports **B.** strainers **C.** storage **D.** faucets

The Chinese and English languages do not have ___15___ rules. In Chinese, for example, verbs do not have tenses, and there is no way to tell whether a noun is singular or ___16___, except from context.

_____ **15. A.** cheerful **B.** later **C.** chemical **D.** similar

_____ **16. A.** adjective **B.** alone **C.** plural **D.** lazy

The deepest ____1____ in the United States is not the Grand Canyon. It is Hells Canyon. The ____2____ at Hells Canyon is greater than the one at the Grand Canyon by half a mile.

_____ 1. **A.** water   **B.** pond   **C.** thinker   **D.** gorge

_____ 2. **A.** flyer   **B.** animal   **C.** chasm   **D.** hill

A small, seaside ____3____ had a terrible problem. It had too many ____4____. These bloodsucking insects bit the tourists. The town solved its problem. It brought in hundreds of dragonflies, which feed on the pests.

_____ 3. **A.** community   **B.** boat   **C.** anchor   **D.** tree

_____ 4. **A.** frogs   **B.** mosquitoes   **C.** woodpeckers   **D.** things

Helicopters are lifted into the air by one or two ____5____ wings. These fast-turning wings whirl through the air. They work against gravity to produce lift. Lift keeps the helicopter ____6____.

_____ 5. **A.** rotating   **B.** slow   **C.** serious   **D.** fixed

_____ 6. **A.** engine   **B.** heavy   **C.** pilot   **D.** aloft

Peter Stuyvesant was one of the most disliked governors in the New World. But he also began the first American fire ____7____ system. He had people ____8____ chimneys for possible fire dangers.

_____ 7. **A.** prevention   **B.** starting   **C.** average   **D.** inning

_____ 8. **A.** launch   **B.** welcome   **C.** inspect   **D.** punch

Before the Wright brothers, there was one ___**9**___ heavier than air that flew under its own power. In 1896 a plane built by S. P. Langley flew at a low ___**10**___ for one and a half minutes. But there was no one on it.

_____ **9.** **A.** feather   **B.** cloud   **C.** aircraft   **D.** artist

_____**10.** **A.** brain   **B.** altitude   **C.** mood   **D.** selection

People are not the cause of most forest fires. Lightning causes the ___**11**___ of all forest fires. Fires thin out the forest and probably ___**12**___ better growth for the rest of the trees.

_____**11.** **A.** decision   **B.** hickory   **C.** nicest   **D.** majority

_____**12.** **A.** bark   **B.** remain   **C.** promote   **D.** speed

If you got a letter from the President, you would own that ___**13**___ piece of mail. But you could not publish it without the President's ___**14**___.

_____**13.** **A.** ancient   **B.** illustrious   **C.** envelope   **D.** brief

_____**14.** **A.** belief   **B.** memory   **C.** permission   **D.** protection

It makes sense that the continents were all once ___**15**___. On a map you can see how the eastern part of South America could ___**16**___ neatly into western Africa.

_____**15.** **A.** connected   **B.** friendly   **C.** water   **D.** think

_____**16.** **A.** obey   **B.** strike   **C.** miss   **D.** nestle

In the 1900s ___**1**___ were built to join bodies of water. Up until that time, people did not have the ___**2**___ knowledge to build such waterways.

_____ **1. A.** canals   **B.** pavements   **C.** sidewalks   **D.** ovens

_____ **2. A.** technical   **B.** water   **C.** shipping   **D.** first

Ransom Olds first ___**3**___ cars in a moving line. It was not Henry Ford. The ___**4**___ of this method was its speed. It more than tripled production.

_____ **3. A.** wrecked   **B.** drove   **C.** assembled   **D.** mailed

_____ **4. A.** advantage   **B.** trouble   **C.** mystery   **D.** doom

Every ___**5**___ knows that some laws protect people. Some laws protect property. Did you know that a higher ___**6**___ of laws protect property?

_____ **5. A.** building   **B.** baby   **C.** lawyer   **D.** tiger

_____ **6. A.** elevator   **B.** proportion   **C.** crime   **D.** judge

Native Americans gathered in Washington, D.C., in 1999. Their ancestors were the area's original ___**7**___. They were there to ___**8**___ land for a museum. The museum will exhibit Native American history, art, and culture.

_____ **7. A.** tourists   **B.** residents   **C.** governors   **D.** coaches

_____ **8. A.** dedicate   **B.** peel   **C.** mention   **D.** wash

Isaac Singer is famous for his improvements to the sewing machine. He became a ___**9**___ at the age of 12. By the time he was 49, his company produced more sewing machines than any other. Singer was also the first person to spend $1 million on ___**10**___.

_____ 9. **A.** machine   **B.** singer   **C.** mechanic   **D.** thimble

_____10. **A.** sorrow   **B.** advertising   **C.** allow   **D.** fish

---

If a ship is in ___**11**___, it can signal another ship for help. The ___**12**___ letters SOS make one of the best-known signals. Flying the national flag upside down is another.

_____11. **A.** waves   **B.** dock   **C.** distress   **D.** peace

_____12. **A.** code   **B.** first   **C.** tall   **D.** windy

---

People dream of making an automobile ___**13**___ from water. The Navy once tested a ___**14**___ that turned water into gas. But the inventor wanted more money than the Navy would pay.

_____13. **A.** fuel   **B.** food   **C.** student   **D.** chalk

_____14. **A.** monkey   **B.** river   **C.** chemical   **D.** very

---

One of the largest groups of flowering plants is the pea family. There are more than twelve thousand ___**15**___. Many plants in this group have very ___**16**___ flowers.

_____15. **A.** leaves   **B.** foods   **C.** species   **D.** shovels

_____16. **A.** attractive   **B.** icy   **C.** confused   **D.** level

Everyone agrees that our ____1____ must be kept clean. But tiny pieces of dust, sea salt, and other matter are what hold water droplets together. These droplets ____2____ as rain. This would not be possible if the air were completely pure.

_____ 1. **A.** bathtubs   **B.** atmosphere   **C.** tires   **D.** fan

_____ 2. **A.** dirty   **B.** darken   **C.** think   **D.** descend

---

If you are ____3____ on a rainy day, pick up a book by Gary Soto. He is an ____4____ of books and stories for young people. His plots and characters seem real.

_____ 3. **A.** wet   **B.** running   **C.** bored   **D.** swimming

_____ 4. **A.** actor   **B.** author   **C.** inventor   **D.** employee

---

In the United States, red ____5____ bob in the water near shore to show boats where to go. "Red-right-returning" is the phrase sailors use to remember where this safe ____6____ is.

_____ 5. **A.** sailors   **B.** fish   **C.** swimmers   **D.** buoys

_____ 6. **A.** boat   **B.** channel   **C.** life   **D.** lock

---

Fannie Lou Hamer wanted all people to be treated as equal ____7____. She wanted the voting system to be fair and represent everyone. She ____8____ groups to get more African Americans to register to vote.

_____ 7. **A.** players   **B.** singers   **C.** citizens   **D.** travelers

_____ 8. **A.** discovered   **B.** ignored   **C.** organized   **D.** counted

Not all settlers at the time of the American Revolution were in favor of the ___9___ of Independence. In fact many settlers fought on ___10___ of the British cause.

_____ **9. A.** Removal **B.** Declaration **C.** Problem **D.** Time

_____ **10. A.** rivers **B.** back **C.** behalf **D.** loss

---

The fierce wasp fights with a huge spider. In the battle the wasp ___11___ her victim with a poisonous sting. The helpless ___12___ is then carried back to the nest. Young wasps eat the spider.

_____ **11. A.** kisses **B.** grins **C.** stuns **D.** protects

_____ **12. A.** man **B.** baby **C.** wasp **D.** prey

An ___13___ digs up the past. This scientist finds out history from objects people have left behind. Ancient garbage dumps hold a ___14___ supply of these objects.

_____ **13. A.** elephant **B.** archaeologist **C.** eagle **D.** ear

_____ **14. A.** pretty **B.** plentiful **C.** quarter **D.** fancy

---

Knights in the movies always seem ___15___ and awkward in their metal suits. But in fact the ___16___ allowed free movement. It weighed less than the equipment a modern soldier carries.

_____ **15. A.** happy **B.** handsome **C.** clumsy **D.** shy

_____ **16. A.** toes **B.** crates **C.** king **D.** armor

UNIT 11

An ___1___ is terrifying. One loosened ___2___ can begin a slide that might end with the whole side of a mountain tumbling down.

_____ 1. A. ache   B. avalanche   C. orchard   D. arm

_____ 2. A. boulder   B. report   C. screw   D. bell

People who are mocked by being called bad names sometimes have the last laugh. They often ___3___ the bad names and make them seem ___4___ instead of shameful. The religious group known as the Quakers, for example, was given that name by enemies.

_____ 3. A. charm   B. advise   C. adopt   D. delay

_____ 4. A. cloudy   B. honorable   C. easy   D. humble

In ___5___ language, when you go ___6___ in a boat, you're heading toward the back of the boat. *Forward* describes the front of the boat.

_____ 5. A. out   B. below   C. down   D. naval

_____ 6. A. land   B. yesterday   C. rude   D. aft

The wood of the ___7___ tree has a red color and a pleasant smell. When people use the wood in closets and chests, the odor seems to keep ___8___ from eating holes in their clothes.

_____ 7. A. corn   B. large   C. cedar   D. tuna

_____ 8. A. children   B. parrots   C. shoes   D. moths

Steck-Vaughn • Comprehension Skills Series

You can take a short journey or a ___9___ one, but this was not always true. The word *journey* at first meant a trip that lasted only one day. It comes from a ___10___ language. *Journee* meant "day" in Old French.

_____ **9. A.** lengthy   **B.** brief   **C.** happy   **D.** boring

_____ **10. A.** funny   **B.** small   **C.** foreign   **D.** daily

There have been many ___11___ in the design of bicycles. The first bicycles had huge iron wheels and were hard to balance. Falls took a heavy ___12___ in broken bones. The "safety" bike had wheels of equal size and was much easier to ride.

_____ **11. A.** wheels   **B.** races   **C.** advances   **D.** chains

_____ **12. A.** appeal   **B.** toll   **C.** decrease   **D.** pride

There are groups to protect trees, whales, and birds. But not many people care about protecting ___13___. Experts believe this lack of ___14___ is a result of these animals' looks as well as the difficulty of keeping them in zoos.

_____ **13. A.** cereal   **B.** reptiles   **C.** shoes   **D.** chalk

_____ **14. A.** concern   **B.** advice   **C.** food   **D.** machines

The ___15___ called the yard was not always 36 inches. It was once the distance between the king's nose and the king's ___16___ hand.

_____ **15. A.** weed   **B.** size   **C.** fence   **D.** measurement

_____ **16. A.** shaking   **B.** final   **C.** extended   **D.** relaxed

All his life, Alexander the Great wanted to ___1___ the entire world. He is said to have ___2___ bitter tears as a boy because he hadn't done it yet.

_____ 1. **A.** awaken   **B.** follow   **C.** conquer   **D.** general

_____ 2. **A.** sewn   **B.** wept   **C.** mocked   **D.** taken

---

Andrew Jackson got his ___3___ because he was strong and hard. The title ___4___ compares him to a tree with the same qualities.

_____ 3. **A.** father   **B.** nickname   **C.** doctor   **D.** office

_____ 4. **A.** Old Hickory   **B.** Old President   **C.** Old Stock
       D. Old Man

In a trial both sides present ___5___ to prove their case. The person accused can be found guilty or ___6___.

_____ 5. **A.** recordings   **B.** songs   **C.** evidence   **D.** mail

_____ 6. **A.** late   **B.** innocent   **C.** thick   **D.** hungry

---

The moon seems huge when it is on the ___7___ and small when it is high in the sky. But your ___8___ is playing tricks on you, because the moon is always the same size.

_____ 7. **A.** plate   **B.** horizon   **C.** sun   **D.** large

_____ 8. **A.** eyesight   **B.** moon   **C.** light   **D.** star

Skateboarding came from surfing. Both sports require a sense of balance and good timing. In special __**9**__ and parks, young skaters do tricks. They turn their boards in complete circles or ride on just two wheels. This sport is now so popular that some cities hold __**10**__ contests.

_____ 9. **A.** rinks   **B.** balloons   **C.** ships   **D.** sand

_____10. **A.** eating   **B.** amateur   **C.** flying   **D.** suit

Perhaps Ben Franklin was America's greatest __**11**__. He began the first library that would __**12**__ books for free.

_____11. **A.** President   **B.** librarian   **C.** talker   **D.** kite

_____12. **A.** write   **B.** publish   **C.** toss   **D.** lend

Nellie Bly wrote about people who were unfair. She once pretended to be __**13**__ to get inside a mental hospital. Her report on life there brought __**14**__.

_____13. **A.** polite   **B.** honest   **C.** insane   **D.** rich

_____14. **A.** selections   **B.** reforms   **C.** jewelry   **D.** actors

The United States has 54 __**15**__ national parks. This park system protects great mountain ranges, sparkling lakes, and cool caves. Some parks are __**16**__ forests. Other parks are historic places.

_____15. **A.** lowly   **B.** magnificent   **C.** dry   **D.** underground

_____16. **A.** vast   **B.** empty   **C.** short   **D.** other

Writing

Read each paragraph. Write a word that makes sense on each line.

I'm sure Mrs. Soliz is the friendliest person in the whole **(1)**_____. Whenever new families move into our apartment building, she's the first one to greet them. She always makes them feel **(2)**_____.

What a terrible day Nick had! Because of a sore throat, he had to stay at home and miss the **(3)**_____. To make matters worse, he couldn't even eat his favorite food, **(4)**_____.

Jill is a pilot. She loves to fly high above the **(5)**_____. From the air, cars look as tiny as **(6)**_____.

To check your answers, turn to page 60.

Read each paragraph. Write a sentence that makes sense on each line.

Eric lives on a wildlife preserve where animals roam freely. Each day he wonders what wild animal might come into his front yard. **(1)** _____

_____. One

morning Eric looked out his window. What a sight!

(2) _____.

Quickly he got his camera. **(3)** _____

_____.

The citizens planned to celebrate the one hundredth anniversary of Springfield. One committee discussed how to decorate the city hall. **(4)** _____

_____. The

program committee couldn't decide what type of

program to have. **(5)** _____

_____.

Then the mayor, Ms. Carter, had a suggestion.

(6) _____.

To check your answers, turn to page 60.

The king cobra is a very dangerous snake. Its bite can kill an elephant in three hours. Most animals attack only when threatened. But the king cobra will attack without being **provoked**.

_____ **1.** In this paragraph, the word **provoked** means
- **A.** rescued
- **B.** given a reason
- **C.** affected
- **D.** poisoned

The tall buildings called skyscrapers might not have been built without the Chicago Fire of 1871. The fire **devastated** the wooden buildings of the city. The first skyscraper was built on the ruins of the fire.

_____ **2.** In this paragraph, the word **devastated** means
- **A.** built
- **B.** designed
- **C.** destroyed
- **D.** sold

Scientists have wondered how the moon came to be. More and more facts **reinforce** the idea that the moon was probably created by a tremendous crash. A planet the size of Mars hit Earth, and the moon broke off from Earth.

_____ **3.** In this paragraph, the word **reinforce** means
- **A.** plan
- **B.** send
- **C.** trim
- **D.** support

On the ocean, distance is measured in **nautical** miles. This kind of mile is about eight hundred feet longer than the mile used for measuring land.

_____ **4.** In this paragraph, the word **nautical** means
- **A.** sea
- **B.** whale
- **C.** shorter
- **D.** probably untrue

If you go to Australia, you will find some **exotic** creatures. The koala looks like a teddy bear. Emus are huge birds that can't fly. There is even a reptile with a blue tongue.

_____ **5.** In this paragraph, the word **exotic** means
   A. tall   **C.** unhappy
   B. friendly   **D.** unusual

Some owls have long, vicious **talons**. They use them to catch mice to eat. They also use them to defend their nests against enemies.

_____ **6.** In this paragraph, the word **talons** means
   A. eyes   **C.** heads
   B. knives   **D.** claws

Plennie L. Wingo was a **pedestrian** who liked to do things differently. He once walked eight thousand miles. He went backward all the way.

_____ **7.** In this paragraph, the word **pedestrian** means
   A. tribe   **C.** pitcher
   B. walker   **D.** flyer

Early computers were huge. Some were as much as one hundred feet long! They took up far too much space for people to use them at home, and their cost was **prohibitive**, too.

_____ **8.** In this paragraph, the word **prohibitive** means
   A. fast   **C.** cheap
   B. too high   **D.** long

They are called the Black Hills of South Dakota, but the word *hills* is a **misnomer**. In fact these are mountains. Some of them rise to an altitude of more than seven thousand feet.

_____ **1.** In this paragraph, the word **misnomer** means
- **A.** compliment
- **B.** wrong name
- **C.** foreign word
- **D.** park

Eli Whitney was **ingenious**. Not only did he invent the cotton gin, but he also produced the first working model of it in only ten days.

_____ **2.** In this paragraph, the word **ingenious** means
- **A.** unhappily married
- **B.** a cloth maker
- **C.** born in the South
- **D.** very clever

People often think that the song about Casey Jones is not true. But the railroad **ballad** tells of a real person. A man named John Luther Jones really saved many lives during a railroad wreck.

_____ **3.** In this paragraph, the word **ballad** means
- **A.** shipping company
- **B.** bravery
- **C.** unsolved mystery
- **D.** poem that is sung

Mae Jemison was the first African American woman in space. She went up in the space shuttle in 1992, and her **objective** was to study the effects of zero gravity on people and animals.

_____ **4.** In this paragraph, the word **objective** means
- **A.** purpose
- **B.** education
- **C.** flight
- **D.** fear

The Chinese food chop suey comes from California, not China. A Chinese person **concocted** a dish out of leftover food in a mining camp. *Chop suey* means "various things."

_____ **5.** In this paragraph, the word **concocted** means
- **A.** threw away
- **B.** made
- **C.** washed out
- **D.** burned up

Cinderella is a **universal** story that exists in many languages. In the French tale, the slipper is made of glass. In some other languages, the shoe is made of fur.

_____ **6.** In this paragraph, the word **universal** means
- **A.** gloomy
- **B.** capital
- **C.** sneaky
- **D.** worldwide

The **sculpture** of the ancient Greeks is praised for the pure look of the white stone figures. But these figures were originally painted brightly by the Greeks.

_____ **7.** In this paragraph, the word **sculpture** means
- **A.** painting
- **B.** carved rock
- **C.** tile floor
- **D.** house

Stop when the light turns red! Then think of Garrett Morgan. He invented the automatic traffic light. He was a **cunning** businessman, too. He used his inventions to start successful companies.

_____ **8.** In this paragraph, the word **cunning** means
- **A.** clever
- **B.** mechanical
- **C.** slow
- **D.** poor

UNIT 15

Many things we use every day were **invented** in the 1800s. Someone from England gave us the bicycle. An American designed the safety pin.

_____ **1.** In this paragraph, the word **invented** means
- **A.** first made
- **B.** finally broken
- **C.** fixed
- **D.** always needed

How would you like a soup made from a bird's nest? Diners in China **consider** bird's nest soup delicious. The right kind of bird's nests are found in caves.

_____ **2.** In this paragraph, the word **consider** means
- **A.** make
- **B.** think
- **C.** take
- **D.** sell

Roberto Clemente was the first Hispanic player to be named to the Baseball Hall of Fame. He won many awards for his **superb** hitting and fielding skills.

_____ **3.** In this paragraph, the word **superb** means
- **A.** poor
- **B.** quick
- **C.** outstanding
- **D.** outdoor

The Trail of Tears was a journey that took place in the United States. White settlers wanted the land where some Native Americans lived. The government forced these native people to move away from their homes. Thousands of them died on the **tragic** trip.

_____ **4.** In this paragraph, the word **tragic** means
- **A.** sad
- **B.** happy
- **C.** rude
- **D.** brief

Steck-Vaughn • Comprehension Skills Series

Yellowstone is the oldest national park in the United States. Congress **established** it as a national park in 1872.

_____ **5.** In this paragraph, the word **established** means
- **A.** cut
- **B.** crowded
- **C.** loved
- **D.** started

Divers uncover many **underwater** secrets. Ancient ships, old cities, and works of art have been found. The sea has hidden some of its treasures for thousands of years.

_____ **6.** In this paragraph, the word **underwater** means
- **A.** on a mountain
- **B.** in the sea
- **C.** near
- **D.** blue

Popcorn is different from other kinds of corn. The **kernels** have hard shells. The water inside each piece of corn turns to steam. The steam makes the pieces of corn swell and pop.

_____ **7.** In this paragraph, the word **kernels** means
- **A.** soldiers
- **B.** cobs
- **C.** flavors
- **D.** seeds

Some batters think that a curve ball drops five feet from home plate. Some have the **view** that it falls ten feet. Some say that a certain star pitcher's curve ball looked as if it were rolling off a table.

_____ **8.** In this paragraph, the word **view** means
- **A.** bat
- **B.** opinion
- **C.** fly
- **D.** eyes

William Shakespeare is thought to be one of the greatest writers of all time. But for all his genius, Shakespeare almost never **created** his own plots. He took them from other sources.

_____ **1.** In this paragraph, the word **created** means
- **A.** colored in
- **B.** borrowed
- **C.** knew the meaning of
- **D.** made up

Most written works can be protected from stealing by a **copyright**. This is not true of titles, however. You could write a book and call it *Moby Dick* or *War and Peace*.

_____ **2.** In this paragraph, the word **copyright** means
- **A.** check against errors
- **B.** type of legal ownership
- **C.** possession of a title
- **D.** kind of strong lock

The creature known as daddy longlegs is not a true spider. Its legs are too long and slender. Its body isn't divided into two **segments** like the body of a true spider.

_____ **3.** In this paragraph, the word **segments** means
- **A.** leaves
- **B.** sections
- **C.** legs
- **D.** eyes

The Declaration of Independence is dated July 4, 1776. But it wasn't **unanimously** approved on that day. It wasn't until later that all members of Congress voted for it.

_____ **4.** In this paragraph, the word **unanimously** means
- **A.** happily
- **B.** in any way
- **C.** without help
- **D.** without a vote against

Some people worry about deer dying of **starvation** during the winter. These people often put hay out for the animals to eat. But deer do not eat hay. In winter they chew on twigs from trees.

_____ **5.** In this paragraph, the word **starvation** means
    A. wandering   **C.** effect of the cold
    B. tameness   **D.** lack of food

It is not against the law to **mutilate** coins or paper money. But you may not want to use it. You can exchange money that has been marked or damaged at any bank.

_____ **6.** In this paragraph, the word **mutilate** means
    A. spend   **C.** cut up or change
    B. save in banks   **D.** play cards with

The baseball team called the Dodgers was originally from Brooklyn. The name is a short form of "Trolley Dodgers." A long time ago, people in Brooklyn had to be **agile** to dodge all the trolley cars.

_____ **7.** In this paragraph, the word **agile** means
    A. in a bus   **C.** baseball fans
    B. quick   **D.** on foot

One of the most dangerous **fictions** people still believe is that a drowning person will rise three times. This belief may cost the life of a swimmer in trouble.

_____ **8.** In this paragraph, the word **fictions** means
    A. untruths   **C.** lifesaving devices
    B. toys   **D.** swimming holes

The mummies of Egypt are very old. So people assume the Egyptians had special ways of **embalming**. Actually it was the dry air that helped preserve their dead.

_____ **1.** In this paragraph, the word **embalming** means
- **A.** making pyramids
- **C.** keeping things alive
- **B.** preventing decay
- **D.** dealing with heat

Modern **appliances** make our lives much easier. Washing machines, dryers, and dishwashers make completing household chores much faster than in the old days. The "good old days" meant hard work!

_____ **2.** In this paragraph, the word **appliances** means
- **A.** movies
- **C.** machines
- **B.** people
- **D.** apples

Lincoln's **proclamation** ending slavery had no immediate effect. His announcement was made in the middle of the Civil War. The South ignored the order.

_____ **3.** In this paragraph, the word **proclamation** means
- **A.** secret message
- **C.** review of the war
- **B.** official, public order
- **D.** loud voice

Across deserts and mountains, Pony Express riders on horseback carried the mail in the Old West. Most riders were young boys. They needed great courage and skill. **Incompetent** riders couldn't do the job!

_____ **4.** In this paragraph, the word **incompetent** means
- **A.** genuine
- **C.** independent
- **B.** poorly skilled
- **D.** experienced

The neighborhood association met every month for several years. But the group **disbanded** when the most active members moved.

_____ **5.** In this paragraph, the word **disbanded** means
- **A.** broke up
- **B.** joined another group
- **C.** got hungry
- **D.** stopped playing music

In her original book, Mary Shelley never called the monster Frankenstein. This wasn't the name of the **supernatural** creature itself. Dr. Frankenstein was the man who created the monster.

_____ **6.** In this paragraph, the word **supernatural** means
- **A.** swimming
- **B.** beyond the laws of nature
- **C.** athletic and fast
- **D.** extremely strong

No snowflake is like any other snowflake. Each one has a **unique** shape of its own.

_____ **7.** In this paragraph, the word **unique** means
- **A.** clear
- **B.** high
- **C.** usual
- **D.** different

Galileo was a famous scientist, but he did not invent the **telescope**. He did improve the device. He was the first person to use it to look at the stars.

_____ **8.** In this paragraph, the word **telescope** means
- **A.** a map of the sea
- **B.** an instrument to magnify
- **C.** a listening device
- **D.** a returnable soda bottle

The idea that Lincoln wrote the Gettysburg Address at the last minute is not true. He began writing the speech two weeks before he had to give it. He **revised** it at least five times.

_____ **1.** In this paragraph, the word **revised** means
    A. sneezed at   **C.** made changes to
    B. lost   **D.** practiced dancing

In open-heart surgery, first an **incision** is made in the skin of the chest. Then the breastbone must be broken. Finally the heart is exposed.

_____ **2.** In this paragraph, the word **incision** means
    A. magnet   **C.** loan
    B. cut   **D.** timber

Finland is a northern country with a very **complex** language. This language is one of the hardest ones to learn. It is also one of the youngest written languages. It was not written down until the nineteenth century.

_____ **3.** In this paragraph, the word **complex** means
    A. difficult   **C.** simple and easy
    B. quick   **D.** pretty

There will probably always be some **controversy** about whether hot food is better than cold food. In terms of food value, there is no argument. Both are equally good for you.

_____ **4.** In this paragraph, the word **controversy** means
    A. cooks   **C.** regions of France
    B. mistake   **D.** difference of opinion

Eating ice cream on a hot day may give you the **illusion** of cooling you off. But in spite of this feeling, eating ice cream really only makes you hotter.

_____ **5.** In this paragraph, the word **illusion** means
- **A.** mistaken idea
- **B.** stains
- **C.** best way
- **D.** inventor

A basic grasp of **aeronautics** will tell you why ice on the wings of a plane is dangerous. The greatest danger is that the ice changes the shape of the wing.

_____ **6.** In this paragraph, the word **aeronautics** means
- **A.** winter
- **B.** the solution to a problem
- **C.** common sense
- **D.** the principles of flight

Frederick Douglass was born a slave. He escaped and became a great speaker. He spent his life **striving** for equal rights for all.

_____ **7.** In this paragraph, the word **striving** means
- **A.** falling
- **B.** struggling
- **C.** leaping
- **D.** wishing

Indentured servants paid for their passage to America with work. Their contracts were torn in half along a jagged, or indented, line. Master and servant each kept a half and then matched halves to prove the contract's **legality**.

_____ **8.** In this paragraph, the word **legality** means
- **A.** trickery
- **B.** daily news
- **C.** hourly wage
- **D.** lawfulness

Some people think that W. C. Fields's **epitaph** reads: "I would rather be in Philadelphia." But this is not true. The funny actor's tombstone says: "W. C. Fields, 1880–1946."

_____ **1.** In this paragraph, the word **epitaph** means
    A. dying words   **C.** most famous joke
    B. last telegram   **D.** words on a grave marker

A farmer can't build a new barn alone. To get help, farmers in the 1800s held barn raisings. The neighbors would **congregate** and work all day to complete the barn.

_____ **2.** In this paragraph, the word **congregate** means
    A. complain   **C.** come together
    B. work alone   **D.** leave

Lions are not as **noble** as people think. For instance, lions sometimes kill for no reason. They do not kill only to get food.

_____ **3.** In this paragraph, the word **noble** means
    A. strong   **C.** good
    B. mean   **D.** fierce

The Constitution does not say that a jury's **verdict** has to be agreed upon by all members. The idea of a jury trial is older than United States laws. It came to the United States from England.

_____ **4.** In this paragraph, the word **verdict** means
    A. dinner   **C.** invitation
    B. chamber   **D.** decision

Japan has the world's oldest national **anthem**. It's called the Kimigayo. People in Japan have been singing it since the ninth century.

_____ **5.** In this paragraph, the word **anthem** means
  A. flag **C.** record
  B. story **D.** song

King Arthur and the Round Table are **legendary**. Lancelot is also a famous figure. But Lancelot was not in the story at first. He was added years later.

_____ **6.** In this paragraph, the word **legendary** means
  A. based on fact **C.** not well understood
  B. in a museum **D.** taken from a myth

The United States city with the largest area is Juneau, Alaska. It became the largest when it **merged** with the town of Douglas, which is on an island. The city covers 3,100 square miles.

_____ **7.** In this paragraph, the word **merged** means
  A. became one **C.** started a war
  B. was sold **D.** sang

Some schools are helping students who speak English to learn Spanish while Spanish-speaking students learn English. They feel it is a good idea to speak **fluently** in both languages.

_____ **8.** In this paragraph, the word **fluently** means
  A. slowly **C.** very well
  B. loudly **D.** not at all

Links is another name for any golf course. But to people who care about **accuracy**, this is wrong. *Links* refers only to a seaside golf course.

_____ **1.** In this paragraph, the word **accuracy** means
- **A.** newness
- **B.** truth
- **C.** style
- **D.** golf bags

Crazy Horse **participated** in the battle known as Custer's Last Stand. Chief Sitting Bull did not. The chief was in the hills away from the battle.

_____ **2.** In this paragraph, the word **participated** means
- **A.** took part
- **B.** watched
- **C.** slept
- **D.** left

Dr. Samuel Johnson was an English writer. Many sayings have been **attributed** to him. He was quoted as saying: "A fishing rod is a stick with a hook at one end and a fool at the other."

_____ **3.** In this paragraph, the word **attributed** means
- **A.** blamed
- **B.** mistaken
- **C.** credited
- **D.** asked

In Robin Hood's time, people kept arrows in a case on their belt. Native Americans **initiated** a new method. They kept their arrows in a case on their back.

_____ **4.** In this paragraph, the word **initiated** means
- **A.** stopped
- **B.** began
- **C.** struggled
- **D.** entertained

Some people think butter is hard on the stomach. It isn't. Your body **digests** butter just as easily as it does margarine.

_____ **5.** In this paragraph, the word **digests** means
- **A.** spreads
- **B.** erases
- **C.** tells the difference
- **D.** breaks down and absorbs

Most people think a **mirage** is something seen by crazy people. In fact, seeing something that is not there can be caused by heat and light.

_____ **6.** In this paragraph, the word **mirage** means
- **A.** crazy person
- **B.** false image
- **C.** storm
- **D.** reflection

A moth begins life in a wormlike form and is later **transformed** into the winged insect. It isn't the moth that eats your clothes. It's the worm.

_____ **7.** In this paragraph, the word **transformed** means
- **A.** changed
- **B.** swallowed
- **C.** dressed
- **D.** dipped

The Chicago Fire is said to have started when Mrs. O'Leary's cow kicked over a lantern. A reporter named Michael Ahern later said that he had **fabricated** this story. He invented it to make his report more exciting.

_____ **8.** In this paragraph, the word **fabricated** means
- **A.** witnessed
- **B.** heard
- **C.** disguised
- **D.** made up

At first the meaning of the word *nice* wasn't nice at all. *Nice* once meant "ignorant." It began to **imply** a more pleasant meaning after the sixteenth century.

_____ **1.** In this paragraph, the word **imply** means
    A. reply   **C.** understand
    B. suggest   **D.** remove

Many people believe that Rome is the oldest **metropolis** in use. But other cities are much older. Rome was founded in 753 B.C. Damascus, Syria, was founded in 3000 B.C.

_____ **2.** In this paragraph, the word **metropolis** means
    A. ruins   **C.** river
    B. government   **D.** city

The opossum **utilizes** its tail for grasping. But baby opossums do not use their tails to hold onto the mother while riding on her back. They use their paws.

_____ **3.** In this paragraph, the word **utilizes** means
    A. uses   **C.** exercises
    B. holds   **D.** stretches

The killer whale deserves its name in the wild. There it destroys dolphins, birds, and fish. But a captured killer whale is **meek** and friendly to people.

_____ **4.** In this paragraph, the word **meek** means
    A. necessary   **C.** quietly obedient
    B. mean   **D.** easily discouraged

Dolly Parton is said to be a modern poet. Her songs give the **essence** of beauty and honesty. "I really don't know anything except what comes out of my heart," she says.

_____ **5.** In this paragraph, the word **essence** means
- **A.** worst part
- **B.** rhyme
- **C.** real meaning
- **D.** smooth edge

Some Native American tribes were **nomads**. They moved from place to place following the buffalo.

_____ **6.** In this paragraph, the word **nomads** means
- **A.** wanderers
- **B.** settlers
- **C.** voters
- **D.** builders

Mark Twain became **bankrupt** by buying a machine for printing. After he lost his money, he paid off his debts by lecturing. He hated to lecture.

_____ **7.** In this paragraph, the word **bankrupt** means
- **A.** unable to work
- **B.** home
- **C.** unable to pay debts
- **D.** into business

Two-headed snakes are rare, but some have been caught. The two heads often attack one another. They also **compete** for food, and they try to swallow one another.

_____ **8.** In this paragraph, the word **compete** means
- **A.** sing
- **B.** leave
- **C.** finish
- **D.** fight

It's a little-known fact that Paul Revere was given **compensation** for his "midnight ride." He earned five shillings for it.

_____ **1.** In this paragraph, the word **compensation** means
- **A.** a horse
- **B.** a saddle
- **C.** words
- **D.** pay

During the Civil War, the South fought against the North. Some families were split. In these cases, it was brother **versus** brother.

_____ **2.** In this paragraph, the word **versus** means
- **A.** against
- **B.** for
- **C.** with
- **D.** because of

Most of the schools in Vietnam were destroyed in the war. Money and materials needed for schools often went to the war effort. In addition, this small nation has a **shortage** of trained teachers. In spite of these problems, most people in Vietnam can read and write.

_____ **3.** In this paragraph, the word **shortage** means
- **A.** theater
- **B.** lack
- **C.** justice
- **D.** delay

The Pennsylvania Dutch don't wear wooden shoes. Their **forebears** came from Germany, not Holland. The mistake is from the word *Deutsch*, which means "German" in the German language.

_____ **4.** In this paragraph, the word **forebears** means
- **A.** wood
- **B.** treats
- **C.** shoes
- **D.** ancestors

Petrified wood isn't wood turned into stone. Minerals in water **penetrate** the wood. Once inside, they take the form of the wood. They remain after the wood rots away.

_____ **5.** In this paragraph, the word **penetrate** means
A. leave   C. drain from
B. smother   D. enter

A trademark is the right a company has to own a brand name. No one else can use a trademark without the permission of the company that is the **proprietor**.

_____ **6.** In this paragraph, the word **proprietor** means
A. company name   C. owner
B. writer   D. same brand

Garbage has always been a problem in big towns. Benjamin Franklin had an idea for a **municipal** program in Philadelphia. He wanted to hire workers to dump garbage into the river.

_____ **7.** In this paragraph, the word **municipal** means
A. hungry   C. real
B. country   D. city

If you go to Yellowstone National Park in winter, you may think you see huge white eggs on the bare ground. They are actually rocks **blanketed** with snow. Snow melts on the warm earth but sticks to the rocks.

_____ **8.** In this paragraph, the word **blanketed** means
A. heated   C. frozen
B. covered   D. shown

There's a house in Massachusetts **fashioned** entirely from newspapers. The walls and roof are pages glued together to form thick boards. The curtains are woven from the funny pages.

_____ **1.** In this paragraph, the word **fashioned** means
- **A.** printed
- **B.** built
- **C.** read
- **D.** clothed

Pepper was once quite rare. In ancient times it was worth its weight in gold. Cities that controlled the buying and selling of spices became rich from the **profitable** trade.

_____ **2.** In this paragraph, the word **profitable** means
- **A.** cheap
- **B.** slow
- **C.** well-paying
- **D.** confusing

In 1980 someone threw a grape more than three hundred feet. A man caught the grape in his mouth. The **site** of this event was a football field in Louisiana.

_____ **3.** In this paragraph, the word **site** means
- **A.** toss
- **B.** place
- **C.** time
- **D.** game

In 1902 a man asked a woman to marry him. She said yes. They decided to wait a few years before they got married. They finally got around to **matrimony** in 1969.

_____ **4.** In this paragraph, the word **matrimony** means
- **A.** talking
- **B.** trying
- **C.** marrying
- **D.** dying

Animals that live in the desert are well protected. Their small bodies help them escape the heat that **scorches** the ground. Some animals stay in tunnels when the hot sun beats down.

_____ **5.** In this paragraph, the word **scorches** means
- **A.** buries
- **B.** waters
- **C.** burns
- **D.** digs

At many beaches people enter contests for building castles from sand. Some of the castles are very **elaborate**. They have towers, windows, and even bridges.

_____ **6.** In this paragraph, the word **elaborate** means
- **A.** sandy
- **B.** short
- **C.** plain
- **D.** fancy

A woman in Australia and a woman in England were pen pals. Their **correspondence** lasted 75 years.

_____ **7.** In this paragraph, the word **correspondence** means
- **A.** letter-writing
- **B.** friends
- **C.** phone calls
- **D.** mailbox

Spanish explorers took gold from the New World aboard their ships. They tried to carry it to Europe. However, many of the ships sank before they reached their **destination**. The old ships still lie beneath the sea. The treasure awaits inside them.

_____ **8.** In this paragraph, the word **destination** means
- **A.** silver
- **B.** goal
- **C.** surface
- **D.** mountain

Marian Anderson began singing when she was eight. Others saw her great talent. They raised money for her to take voice lessons. As she grew up, she became famous. This **extraordinary** singer was the first African American to sing with the Metropolitan Opera.

_____ **1.** In this paragraph, the word **extraordinary** means
- **A.** soft
- **B.** educated
- **C.** beginning
- **D.** remarkable

Many farmers do not like crows. These birds are **notorious** for eating corn. However, crows really help farmers. They eat harmful insects.

_____ **2.** In this paragraph, the word **notorious** means
- **A.** hidden
- **B.** loved
- **C.** widely known
- **D.** starved

It is not quite true that anybody can be President of the United States. To be **eligible**, a person must be born a United States citizen and be at least 35 years old.

_____ **3.** In this paragraph, the word **eligible** means
- **A.** qualified
- **B.** envied
- **C.** denied
- **D.** defeated

The goosefish is a **weird** sight, with its mouth as wide as a dinner plate! Sometimes this fish is called the "allmouth."

_____ **4.** In this paragraph, the word **weird** means
- **A.** pleasant
- **B.** strange
- **C.** frequent
- **D.** unfriendly

It is hard to imagine not knowing the number zero. But people long ago were **reluctant** to treat nothing as something. They used the other numbers for hundreds of years. Then they finally began to use zero. They could solve many more problems!

_____ **5.** In this paragraph, the word **reluctant** means
    A. listening   **C.** unwilling
    B. ruining   **D.** paying

Henry Ford was **obsessed** with soybeans. Ford kept soybean milk at home. He once wore a soybean suit. He also spoke constantly about different uses for the vegetable.

_____ **6.** In this paragraph, the word **obsessed** means
    A. against using   **C.** slightly fond of
    B. puzzled by   **D.** completely absorbed by

Some people think that the Morse code should be called the Vail code. Alfred Vail, Morse's **associate**, improved the telegraph. But his partner, Morse, held all the legal rights to the machine.

_____ **7.** In this paragraph, the word **associate** means
    A. employee   **C.** thief
    B. son   **D.** coworker

The continental United States now has four time zones, and those are enough to **baffle** most people. Imagine how confusing it must have been before 1883. Then there were about one hundred time zones.

_____ **8.** In this paragraph, the word **baffle** means
    A. time   **C.** anger
    B. confuse   **D.** change

The number of rattles on a rattlesnake is not a **reliable** way to tell its age. It isn't a good measure because snakes grow rattles at different rates.

_____ **1.** In this paragraph, the word **reliable** means
    A. human   **C.** sure
    B. foolish   **D.** mathematical

Phillipe Petite performed a daring **aerial** feat. He strung a rope between the twin towers of New York's World Trade Center. Then he walked across the tightrope.

_____ **2.** In this paragraph, the word **aerial** means
    A. lazy   **C.** unlucky
    B. in the air   **D.** nightly

Can you find your way home by smell? Bees can because each beehive has its own **unmistakable** smell. Bees sense it with their antennae and follow it home.

_____ **3.** In this paragraph, the word **unmistakable** means
    A. obvious   **C.** pleasing
    B. unpleasant   **D.** sweet

Richard the Lion-Hearted is known as a king who was concerned for his people. This picture is false. His fame as a brave soldier, on the other hand, is **justified** by his deeds.

_____ **4.** In this paragraph, the word **justified** means
    A. supported   **C.** denied
    B. not believed   **D.** substituted

The wise man Confucius said that people should lead good lives. He said, "A superior person knows what is right. An **inferior** person knows what is profitable."

_____ **5.** In this paragraph, the word **inferior** means

A. shining   **C.** thinking

B. working   **D.** unworthy

If you dislike wet weather, go to the Atacama Desert in Chile. Some parts of this **parched** South American land have never recorded any rainfall.

_____ **6.** In this paragraph, the word **parched** means

A. rainy   **C.** cold

B. dry   **D.** southern

Planting trees in cities was not always a popular idea. Benjamin Franklin spoke out against having trees in front of houses. He thought the trees would **hinder** the work of firefighters if the houses caught fire.

_____ **7.** In this paragraph, the word **hinder** means

A. speed up   **C.** help

B. slow down   **D.** improve

The library information desk receives many **inquiries**. There are many different ways to find the answers.

_____ **8.** In this paragraph, the word **inquiries** means

A. damages   **C.** licenses

B. questions   **D.** products

Writing

Read each paragraph. Write a word that makes sense on each line.

Reggie was painting his **(1)** _____.

He hoped he had enough **(2)** _____

to finish the job he had started.

Josefina decided to hold a yard sale this

(3) _____. She invited all her

(4) _____ to bring their stuff, too.

Keisha is the oldest in her family. She is in charge of

(5) _____ at her home. At night Keisha

loves to **(6)** _____.

To check your answers, turn to page 60.

Steck-Vaughn • Comprehension Skills Series

Read each paragraph. Write a sentence that makes sense on each line.

Luisa lived on a farm. Her cousin Ana was coming to visit, and Luisa wanted her to have a good time. What would Ana enjoy doing? **(1)** _____

_____ .

Luisa thought about the things she did. **(2)** _____

_____ .

Now she knew what she and Ana could do.

(3) _____ .

The hamster's cage door was open. The cage was empty. Where could the hamster be? **(4)** _____

_____ .

Akeem remembered a story about a hamster.

(5) _____ .

Now he knew where he would look next.

(6) _____ .

To check your answers, turn to page 60.

Check Yourself

Working with Context, Page 4
2. B
3. D

To check your answers to pages 6–29, see page 61.

Writing, Page 30
Possible answers include:

1. neighborhood or world
2. welcome or comfortable
3. game or party
4. pizza or tacos
5. clouds or city
6. toys or ants

Writing, Page 31
Possible answers include:

1. It might be an elephant. It might be a lion.
2. A baby giraffe was eating leaves. Some chimps were eating bananas.
3. He shot a whole roll of film. He took many pictures.
4. They talked about making banners. They talked about getting old photos of the city.
5. They might do a play. They might have a band concert.
6. She suggested fireworks. She suggested a parade.

To check your answers to pages 32–57, see page 62.

Writing, Page 58
Possible answers include:

1. house or room
2. time or paint
3. Saturday or weekend
4. neighbors or friends
5. meals or planning
6. cook or organize

Writing, Page 59
Possible answers include:

1. She might like to milk the cow. She might like to gather eggs.
2. She always fed the chickens. She helped clean the stables.
3. They could play with the baby goats. They could ride horses.
4. It might be on the desk. It might be on the bookshelf.
5. The hamster liked dark places. The hamster was always looking for food.
6. He would look under the bed. He would look in the kitchen.

Check Yourself

Unit 1 pp. 6–7	Unit 2 pp. 8–9	Unit 3 pp. 10–11	Unit 4 pp. 12–13	Unit 5 pp. 14–15	Unit 6 pp. 16–17	Unit 7 pp. 18–19	Unit 8 pp. 20–21	Unit 9 pp. 22–23	Unit 10 pp. 24–25	Unit 11 pp. 26–27	Unit 12 pp. 28–29
1. B	1. B	1. A	1. D	1. D	1. A	1. B	1. D	1. A	1. B	1. B	1. C
2. A	2. D	2. B	2. B	2. C	2. B	2. A	2. C	2. A	2. D	2. A	2. B
3. B	3. C	3. C	3. C	3. A	3. B	3. C	3. A	3. C	3. C	3. C	3. B
4. A	4. A	4. A	4. A	4. B	4. B	4. D	4. B	4. A	4. B	4. B	4. A
5. A	5. B	5. B	5. B	5. B	5. C	5. C	5. A	5. C	5. D	5. D	5. C
6. D	6. B	6. D	6. A	6. C	6. D	6. A	6. D	6. B	6. B	6. D	6. B
7. B	7. C	7. B	7. D	7. C	7. D	7. B	7. A	7. B	7. C	7. C	7. B
8. C	8. D	8. C	8. A	8. A	8. C	8. D	8. C	8. A	8. C	8. D	8. A
9. D	9. B	9. B	9. C	9. C	9. C	9. C	9. C	9. C	9. B	9. A	9. A
10. A	10. D	10. B	10. A	10. D	10. C	10. B	10. B	10. B	10. C	10. C	10. B
11. C	11. A	11. D	11. D	11. D	11. C	11. C	11. D	11. C	11. C	11. C	11. B
12. A	12. B	12. D	12. C	12. A	12. A	12. B	12. C	12. A	12. D	12. B	12. D
13. B	13. D	13. C	13. B	13. D	13. C	13. A	13. B	13. A	13. B	13. B	13. C
14. D	14. C	14. B	14. C	14. C	14. D	14. C	14. C	14. C	14. B	14. A	14. B
15. C	15. D	15. B	15. A	15. D	15. A	15. D	15. A	15. C	15. C	15. D	15. B
16. C	16. A	16. C	16. D	16. A	16. B	16. C	16. D	16. A	16. D	16. C	16. A

Unit 13 pp. 32–33	Unit 14 pp. 34–35	Unit 15 pp. 36–37	Unit 16 pp. 38–39	Unit 17 pp. 40–41	Unit 18 pp. 42–43	Unit 19 pp. 44–45	Unit 20 pp. 46–47	Unit 21 pp. 48–49	Unit 22 pp. 50–51	Unit 23 pp. 52–53	Unit 24 pp. 54–55	Unit 25 pp. 56–57
1. B	1. B	1. A	1. D	1. B	1. C	1. D	1. B	1. B	1. D	1. B	1. D	1. C
2. C	2. D	2. B	2. B	2. C	2. B	2. C	2. A	2. D	2. A	2. C	2. C	2. B
3. D	3. D	3. C	3. B	3. B	3. A	3. C	3. C	3. A	3. B	3. B	3. A	3. A
4. A	4. A	4. A	4. D	4. B	4. D	4. D	4. B	4. C	4. D	4. C	4. B	4. A
5. D	5. B	5. D	5. D	5. A	5. A	5. D	5. D	5. C	5. D	5. C	5. C	5. D
6. D	6. D	6. B	6. C	6. B	6. D	6. D	6. B	6. A	6. C	6. D	6. D	6. B
7. B	7. B	7. D	7. B	7. D	7. B	7. A	7. A	7. C	7. D	7. A	7. D	7. B
8. B	8. A	8. B	8. A	8. B	8. D	8. C	8. D	8. D	8. B	8. B	8. B	8. B